3.5 02

P9-DDI-133

DISCARD

Georgia, My State
Habitats

Atlantic Ocean

by Doraine Bennett

STATE
STANDARDS
PUBLISHING ®

Your State • Your Standards • Your Grade Level

Dear Educators, Librarians and Parents . . .

Thank you for choosing the *"Georgia, My State"* Series! We have designed this series to support the Georgia Department of Education's Georgia Performance Standards for elementary level Georgia studies. Each book in the series has been written at appropriate grade level as measured by the ATOS Readability Formula for Books (Accelerated Reader), the Lexile Framework for Reading, and the Fountas & Pinnell Benchmark Assessment System for Guided Reading. Photographs and/or illustrations, captions, and other design elements have been included to provide supportive visual messaging to enhance text comprehension. Glossary and Word Index sections introduce key new words and help young readers develop skills in locating and combining information.

We wish you all success in using the *"Georgia, My State"* Series to meet your student or child's learning needs. For additional sources of information, see www.georgiaencyclopedia.org.

Jill Ward, President

Publisher
State Standards Publishing, LLC
1788 Quail Hollow
Hamilton, GA 31811
USA
1.866.740.3056
www.statestandardspublishing.com

Library of Congress Cataloging-in-Publication Data
Bennett, Doraine, 1953-
  Atlantic Ocean / by Doraine Bennett.
    p. cm. -- (Georgia, my state. Habitats)
  Includes index.
  ISBN-13: 978-1-935077-34-3 (hardcover)
  ISBN-10: 1-935077-34-1 (hardcover)
  ISBN-13: 978-1-935077-39-8 (pbk.)
  ISBN-10: 1-935077-39-2 (pbk.)
  1. Seashore ecology--Georgia--Juvenile literature. 2. Seashore ecology--South Atlantic Ocean--Juvenile literature. 3. Marine animals--Georgia--Juvenile literature. 4. Marine animals--South Atlantic Ocean--Juvenile literature. I. Title.
  QH105.G4B458 2009
  577.7'348--dc22
                            2009012570

Table of Contents

Plankton

This right whale is eating plankton.

Georgia Atlantic Ocean

A storm petrel stirs up the water to find plankton.

The Atlantic Ocean is home to some of the largest and smallest plants and animals in the world.

Which Ocean is Near Georgia?

A storm petrel skims across the waves of the Atlantic Ocean. Its webbed feet patter across the surface. The petrel is stirring up the water to find **plankton** to eat. A right whale swims with its mouth open. The whale catches plankton and tiny shell animals for a meal. Plankton are the smallest plants and animals in the ocean. They are food for many **aquatic** animals. Aquatic animals live in water.

The Atlantic Ocean is the saltiest ocean in the world. It is the **habitat** for some of the smallest and largest plants and animals in the world. A habitat is a place where plants and animals live. The ocean provides everything they need to survive.

It's a Fact!

Some plankton are so small you need a microscope to see them. A microscope makes tiny things big enough to see.

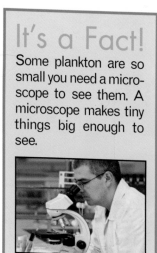

Tides are caused by the pull of gravity from the moon and sun.

This spotted dolphin is swimming in the ocean current.

This boat floats when the tide is up. It is stranded on the beach when the tide is down.

The ocean is always moving.

Constant Motion!

The Atlantic Ocean is always moving. Waves roll across the surface. **Currents** move the water slowly from place to place. Currents are like rivers deep in the ocean. **Tides** raise and lower the water in giant swells. Tides are the rising and falling of the water levels of the ocean. They are caused by the pull of **gravity** from the moon and sun. Gravity is the pull of things toward each other. It's what makes things fall to the ground.

Dolphins and swordfish leap from the water. They are always moving, too!

Dolphins and swordfish stay on the move!

7

The ocean is not very deep over the continental shelf.

You can wade in a long way!

Mountains

Piedmont

Coastal Plain

Marsh and Swamp →

← Coast

ATLANTIC OCEAN

The coast is the place where land meets the ocean.

Georgia's coast is on the Atlantic Ocean.

Life on the Continental Shelf

Georgia's **coast** is on the Atlantic Ocean. A coast is the place where land meets the ocean. At the coast, the land slopes down gradually into the ocean. This part of the ocean floor is called the **continental shelf**. Water over the continental shelf is not very deep. You can wade in a long way. Sunlight reaches to the sandy bottom here. Ocean plants need sunlight to grow.

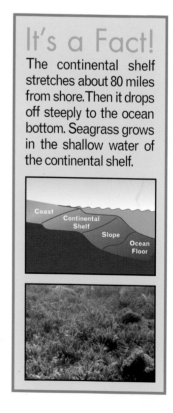

It's a Fact!

The continental shelf stretches about 80 miles from shore. Then it drops off steeply to the ocean bottom. Seagrass grows in the shallow water of the continental shelf.

Sea Slug

Jellyfish

Black Sea Bass

Lobster

Sponges

Almost every inch of Gray's Reef is covered with ocean plants and animals.

Gray's Reef

Gray's Reef is about twenty miles from the coast of Georgia. Gray's Reef is a large area of rock on the continental shelf.

The reef is home to over 150 types of fish. Corals, sea stars, and sponges attach themselves to the rock. Snails called sea slugs crawl on the rocks and corals. Crabs and lobsters hide under the rocky ledges. Fish and jellyfish swim overhead. Almost every inch of Gray's Reef is covered with ocean plants and animals.

Sea Star

Loggerheads crush oysters and other shells with their strong jaws.

Loggerhead turtles have flippers instead of legs. They swim fast!

Loggerhead turtles live near Gray's Reef.

Reptiles in the Ocean

Loggerhead turtles live near Gray's Reef. Turtles are **reptiles**. Reptiles are animals that are covered with scales or shells.

Loggerhead turtles are sea turtles. They eat shellfish, like clams and oysters. The loggerhead turtle has strong jaws. Its jaws crush the shells. Sea turtles have flippers instead of legs. They are fast swimmers.

It's a Fact!

Once, shrimp boats caught turtles in their nets. The turtles would drown. Now, shrimp nets have a special door that opens when a turtle pushes against it. It lets the turtle escape.

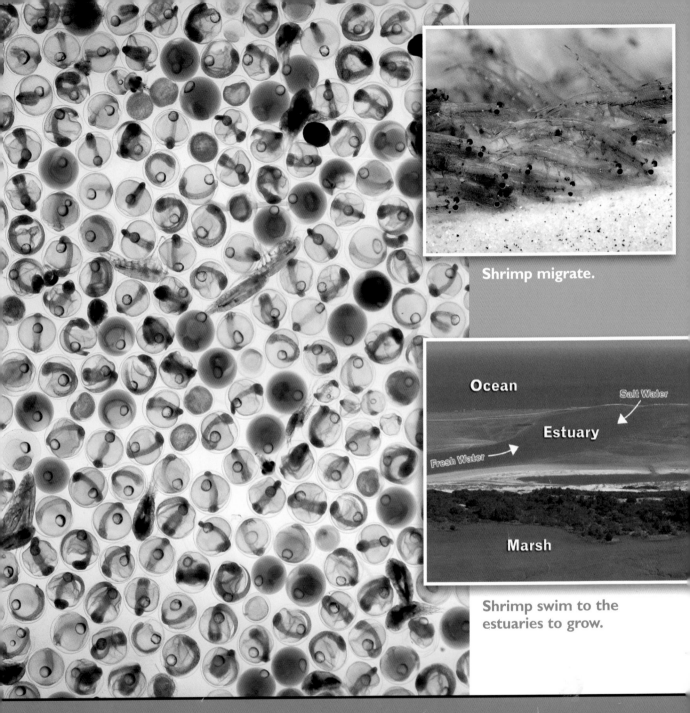

Shrimp migrate.

Ocean

Estuary

Salt Water

Fresh Water

Marsh

Shrimp swim to the estuaries to grow.

Shrimp lay their eggs in the ocean water.

Shrimp!

Shrimp lay their eggs in the ocean water. The eggs float on the current. They hatch in about one day.

The tiny shrimp eat plankton. They **migrate**. They move from one place to another when they are large enough to swim. They migrate to the **estuaries**. Estuaries are places where fresh water from rivers and creeks meets salt water from the ocean. The estuaries help protect the young shrimp.

Shrimp live in the estuaries until they are fully grown. Then they swim back to the ocean to lay their eggs.

It's a Fact!

Shrimp are Georgia's main seafood crop. Over 500 shrimp boats sail from Georgia's coast every year to catch shrimp.

Mackerel

Shark

Barb →

Stingray

Grouper

Red Snapper

These red snappers are hiding in Gray's Reef!

All Kinds of Fish in the Ocean

Bony fish live in the Atlantic Ocean. They have skeletons made of bones. Bony fish are good to eat. Black sea bass, grouper, and mackerel are bony fish. Red snapper and flounder are bony fish, too. Sharks and stingrays don't have hard bones. They have skeletons made of **cartilage**. Cartilage is flexible. You have cartilage in your nose and ears.

Sharks are **predators**. They hunt other animals for food. They have sharp teeth! The stingray has a long tail with sharp barbs on it. The stingray uses its barb to defend itself.

It's a Fact!

The flounder uses **camouflage** to hide from predators. Camouflage helps animals look like their surroundings. Can you see the flounder?

People are very small compared to a right whale!

The warm water off the Georgia coast helps right whale calves survive.

Right Whale

Loggerhead turtles are endangered, too.

Right whales migrate to the Georgia coast in winter.

Endangered Species

The right whale is one of the largest **mammals** in the ocean. Mammals nurse their young with milk, like humans. Right whales are big and slow. Whale hunters killed many right whales. They are an endangered species. They are protected so that they don't cease to exist, or become **extinct**.

In winter, right whales migrate to the ocean near Georgia. They move from the colder parts of the ocean to warmer water. They give birth to their calves here. The warmer water helps the calves survive until they grow bigger.

It's a Fact!

Whale hunters killed many whales. They ate the whale meat. They made whale oil to burn in their lamps. Today, there are only about 300 right whales in the world.

Northern Gannet

Greater Shearwater

Storm Petrels

Young Northern Gannet

This young northern gannet will be brightly colored when it grows.

Ocean Birds

The northern gannet lives over the Atlantic Ocean. It can dive 70 feet under the water to catch fish! Greater shearwaters skim the surface of the water. Their wings stretch out 4 feet wide! Storm petrels are also common over the Atlantic Ocean. They eat plankton on the ocean surface. At night, they float on the water and sleep.

These birds are sea birds. They spend most of their lives living over the ocean!

It's a Fact!

Sea birds only come on land to breed and take care of their young.

Glossary

aquatic – Animals and plants that live in the water.

bony fish – Fish that have skeletons made of bones.

camouflage – A way an animal hides by looking like its surroundings.

cartilage – Flexible bones, like the bones in human noses and ears.

coast – The place where the ocean meets the land.

continental shelf – Land that slopes down gradually from the coast.

currents – The movement of ocean water, like rivers in the ocean.

estuaries – Bodies of water where fresh water from rivers and creeks mixes with salt water from the ocean.

extinct – No longer existing.

gravity – The pull of things toward each other. Gravity makes things fall to the ground.

habitat – A place where plants and animals live.

mammals – Animals that nurse their young with milk.

migrate – The movement of animals from one place to another.

plankton – Small plants and animals in the ocean that other animals eat for food.

predators – Animals that hunt other animals for food.

reptiles – Animals that are covered with scales, like lizards, or shells, like turtles.

tides – The rising and lowering of the waters of the ocean.

Word Index

Image Credits

About the Author

Doraine Bennett has a degree in professional writing from Columbus State University in Columbus, Georgia, and has been writing and teaching writing for over twenty years. She has authored numerous articles in magazines for both children and adults and is the editor of the National Infantry Association's *Infantry Bugler* magazine. Doraine enjoys reading and writing books and articles for children. She lives in Georgia with her husband, Cliff.